Young
Christopher Columbus

Discoverer of New Worlds

A Troll First-Start Biography

by Eric Carpenter
illustrated by John Himmelman

Troll Associates

Library of Congress Cataloging-in-Publication Data

Carpenter, Eric.
    Young Christopher Columbus: discoverer of the new worlds / by
Eric Carpenter; illustrated by John Himmelman.
        p.   cm.—(First-start biographies)
    Summary: An easy-to-read biography of the famous explorer who
became one of the first people to sail to America.
    ISBN 0-8167-2526-8 (lib. bdg.)   ISBN 0-8167-2527-6 (pbk.)
    1. Columbus, Christopher—Juvenile literature.   2. Explorers—
America—Biography—Juvenile literature.   3. Explorers—Spain—
Biography—Juvenile literature.   4. America—Discovery and
exploration—Spanish—Juvenile literature.   [1. Columbus,
Christopher.   2. Explorers.   3. America—Discovery and exploration—
Spanish.]   I. Himmelman, John, ill.   II. Title.   III. Series.
E111.C33   1992
970.01 '5—dc20
[B]   91-24975

Christopher Columbus was one of the first people to sail to America.

Christopher was born in Genoa, Italy in 1451. Genoa was a busy seaport. Ships from all over the world sailed in and out of its harbor.

Christopher's father was a weaver. Christopher often helped in his father's shop. He was a quiet boy who liked to daydream.

More than anything, Christopher loved
the sea. Whenever he could, he went
to the harbor to watch the ships.
"One day I will sail to faraway lands,"
he said.

6

When Columbus was about 19, he had a chance to make his dreams come true. He joined the crew of a ship and sailed to many places.

In 1477, Columbus moved to Portugal.
He learned that King John II of
Portugal wanted someone to sail to the
"Indies." The "Indies" at the time
meant India, China, the East Indies,
and Japan.

There were many riches in the Indies.
But getting them to Portugal by land
took a long time. King John thought it
would be quicker to go to the Indies
by ship.

11

Columbus wanted to sail to the Indies.
He planned his trip carefully.

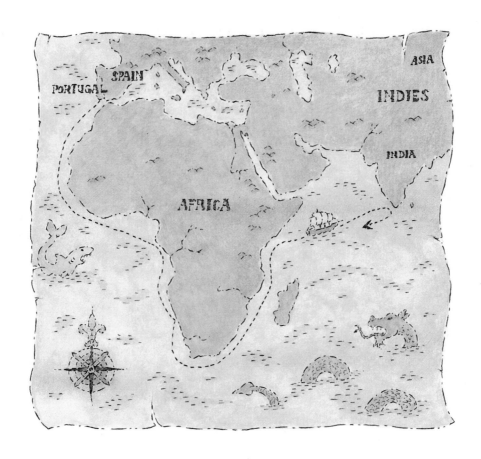

Most people thought the fastest way to the Indies was to sail east around the tip of Africa. But this was a long and dangerous voyage.

13

Columbus thought that sailing *west* would be faster. He told King John about his plan. He hoped the king would give him money for the trip.

But King John said no. He did not
think Columbus' plan would work.

Columbus was disappointed. But he
did not give up. He brought his plan to
Queen Isabella and King Ferdinand
of Spain.

Unfortunately, Spain was fighting a war. Columbus had to wait 7 years for an answer! Luckily, it was the answer he had been hoping for. The queen said yes!

On August 3, 1492, Columbus began his great adventure. He left Spain with 3 ships, the *Niña*, the *Pinta*, and the *Santa Maria*.

The voyage was long. For weeks and weeks the 3 ships sailed across the Atlantic Ocean. The crew wanted to turn back. But Columbus sailed on.

Finally, on October 12, a sailor on the *Pinta* saw a wonderful sight. "Land!" he shouted. "Land!"

Columbus believed he had reached the
Indies. So when the island's people
came to meet him, Columbus named
them *Indians*. But he was really on
San Salvador, near Florida.

Columbus explored many islands. He met friendly natives and found gold and other gifts to bring back to the king and queen of Spain.

Columbus returned to Spain on March
15, 1493. King Ferdinand and Queen
Isabella welcomed him home as a
great hero. And they gave him money
to return to "the New World."

Columbus made 3 more trips to the
New World. He explored many
new places.

Columbus returned to Spain in 1504.
Two years later Columbus died.

Even though Columbus never reached
the Indies, he made Europeans aware
of a whole new world.

Christopher Columbus was an explorer
who opened new horizons.

32